Clothes from History to Make and Wear

BIBLICAL CLOTHES

Text: **Suzi Clarke**
Patterns: **Carole Hersee**
Paintings: **Carol Wainwright**

YOUNG LIBRARY

First published in 1989 by

Young Library Ltd
The Old Brushworks
56 Pickwick Road
Corsham, Wiltshire SN13 9BX

ISBN 0 946003 84 X

Printed and bound in Hong Kong

CONTENTS

INTRODUCTION

The Bible spans thousands of years and many different peoples and countries. It would be impossible to describe all the clothing styles, so we have chosen a few to illustrate what was worn in and around Bible lands from about 2000 B.C. to after the time of Christ.

The patterns in this book are based on written descriptions, on statues and wall-paintings, and on pictures on pottery and similar objects. You can see many of these things yourself in museums and in books. However, we have also had to make assumptions sometimes, and accept the traditional view of what these people wore.

The costumes described in this book might be called by different names elsewhere, so be careful if you are working from more than one book.

Fabrics

First we look at the Hebrews, who lived originally in Israel. Their clothes did not change much for centuries, and the same kind of robes would have been worn for the whole of this period.

Hebrew clothes were very simple. They were probably made of soft wool or linen and coloured with vegetable dyes. Cloth was woven by hand on a loom. Sewing was also done by hand, as there were no sewing machines in those days. Some fabrics were plain; others had simple patterns woven or embroidered into them. It is quite easy to find modern fabrics which look like the cloth made at this time. Old blankets, especially coloured ones, are particularly good, but other suitable materials can be bought at most fabric shops.

The tribes of Israel were in exile in Egypt from about 1750 to about 1320 B.C. They lived under the rule of the Pharaohs (kings) of Egypt. The clothes were made of light-weight material, probably linen, because of the hot climate. Members of the royal family and the royal court, rich people, and priests, often wore finely pleated garments.

You can make Egyptian-style clothes from sheeting or one of the many lining materials available. Patterns can be drawn or painted on the material with fabric pens or paints. You can use painted cardboard and pasta shapes to make elaborate jewellery and headdresses. Craft shops often sell beads which can be threaded on string or shoe laces to make effective necklaces.

The Assyrian and Babylonian kingdoms were to the east of Egypt and Palestine, in what are now Iran, Iraq, and Syria. The people's clothes were quite different from the clothes worn by the Hebrews and the Egyptians. Many wore very rich robes, trimmed with fringes. The robes often had patterns woven into the borders. The clothes would probably have been made of soft wool or linen. You can copy them in the same modern fabrics. The fringe could be made from lampshade trimming. You can make macramé belts which are very similar to the knotted girdles worn in those days.

The best-known period of ancient Greece is about 600−300 B.C. The Greeks wore robes of fine linen or wool, mostly in pale colours, and often with geometric patterns woven along the edges. These robes were very plain. Often they were just straight lengths of fabric pinned on the shoulder and along the arms, and tied with a girdle. There was very little difference between the styles worn by men and women.

A robe worn by men, women, and children was called a chiton. It could be worn long, medium length below the knee, or short. Women also wore a long robe called a peplos which had some of the fabric folded over at the top to make a kind of deep collar.

Plain sheeting is the most suitable fabric for these robes. They can be decorated along the edges with fabric pens or paints, perhaps using potato or lino prints (see below). The garments need very little sewing and can be held together with brooches or buttons.

The Roman Empire came after the Greek Empire. At first, Roman robes were very similar to those worn by the Greeks. In later styles, the pieces of cloth were longer and were draped or folded round the body in different ways. These robes were called togas. They were worn over a simple tunic similar to the Greek tunic. The Romans used the same type of material as the Greeks, so plain sheeting is the best modern fabric to use.

There was little difference between the styles of men and women, but colours and patterns showed what kind of person the wearer was. For example an ordinary Roman citizen was only allowed to wear natural coloured wool with no fancy edging, while a 14−16 year old boy could wear white with a band of scarlet or purple along the straight edge.

Roman soldiers wore armour made of leather or metal. You can make armour from cardboard or one of the modern synthetic leathers. Loose knitting in thick wool makes good chain mail. Paint sprays can make all of these look like metal if they are used with care and the instructions are followed properly.

The Byzantine Empire took over power from the Roman Empire in about A.D. 330, and survived for over 1,000 years. The Byzantine people also wore very simple tunics and draped robes, but in bright and patterned fabrics. It is easy to copy these in modern fabrics.

Throughout the period of the Bible, people went barefoot or wore sandals. Hair seems to have been worn long in the southern and eastern Mediterranean, and short in Greece and Rome, but variations could be found everywhere. Assyrian wall reliefs show men with beards. The Egyptian nobility seem to have worn artificial beards for special oc-

casions. Headdresses were often just a piece of fabric which was wrapped around the head in different ways depending on the country or the wishes of the wearer. Clothes for men and women were often very similar, and children usually wore less elaborate versions of their parents' clothes. There was little difference between boys' and girls' clothes. Throughout this time clothes were simple and needed very little sewing.

We have also included a pattern for angel's wings which can be used for Nativity plays.

FABRIC PRINTING

This section gives a few ideas for printing fabrics. If you want to know more, there are several books which deal with the subject in detail. Instructions are usually supplied with fabric paints and dyes.

Potato printing: You will need fabric dyes, a sharp knife, a small piece of felt or several thicknesses of kitchen paper, and a potato.

Cut a potato in half and trim it to the required shape. Cut a design on the flat surface. The lines must be very clear. A simple design is most effective.

Fold the felt or kitchen paper to make a pad, and pour some dye on to it. Dry the cut edge of the potato, and press it on to the pad, then on to the fabric. Allow the print to dry thoroughly.

Lino Blocks: Cut a design on a piece of lino and use in the same way as potato prints. It can be used for more delicate patterns than potato prints, because you can cut finer detail on to lino.

Stencils: Cut a simple shape in the middle of a piece of thick card or stencil paper. Position it over fabric and paint fabric through it. Several stencils can be taped together and sprayed to make a bigger pattern. The surrounding material should be covered carefully to avoid spraying the wrong areas.

Other ideas: Washing-up sponges make good printing blocks for very simple, blurred patterns; they can be cut into shapes with scissors or a knife. A very delicate pattern can be made by laying lace or a fabric with

Hebrew Man and Woman
He wears a full length basic tunic with tunic sleeves.
Over the tunic he wears a sleeveless, open coat. She
wears a gathered robe with gathered sleeves over a full
length basic tunic with narrow sleeves.

an openwork design over the main fabric, and spraying through it. You can make patterns by painting glue on to the fabric and sprinkling coloured glitter over it.

PLEATING

The best fabric for pleating is a very fine type such as lawn or silk. Some very fine lining fabrics may be suitable. It is a good idea to practise with a small piece of the fabric to see if it will pleat properly.

Wet fabric thoroughly. Work across the fabric from selvedge to selvedge. Hold one edge of the fabric between the thumb and the rest of the hand, and begin pushing the fabric along the fingers into the fist. The raw edge should stand up about 2.5cm. Continue until all the fabric is held tightly in the fist.

Wrap an elastic band tightly round top of the material, about 2.5cm from the raw edge. Repeat at other end of fabric.

Two people are needed now, one to hold each end of the fabric. Each person twists the fabric in opposite directions, pulling it tightly all the time. Twist until the fabric knots up on itself. Without letting go, tuck the knotted fabric into the leg of an old pair of tights, or tie in several places.

Hang in a hot place to dry (over a radiator is ideal). The fabric can take up to a week to dry thoroughly. Make sure it is completely dry before undoing it, or the pleats will drop out. Do not stretch the pleats when using the fabric. Lay the pattern on as though it were flat fabric.

Pleating uses a great deal of fabric, so be sure to make enough. You can join widths before pleating. Use a very narrow seam.

Patterns

A dress pattern is a plan drawing of the garment to be made. It is drawn to the same size as the garment, then pinned to the fabric and used as a guide in cutting the required shapes.

All the patterns in this book are drawn on to a grid pattern of blue squares. Each side of a square represents two centimetres. There-

fore, if the pattern shows a line extending for seven squares, it means it should be fourteen centimetres in length.

All measurements throughout are in centimetres, marked 'cm'.

This is the key to the various line markings on the patterns:

— — — — — — —

fold of fabric

— — — — — —

lengthening or shortening line

— · — · — · — ·

extension line

· · · · · · · · · · ·

alternative cutting line

Most patterns are shown in two sizes — Size A in black, and Size B in red, according to the measurements below:

	GIRLS		BOYS	
	SIZE A	SIZE B	SIZE A	SIZE B
CHEST	72.5	81	71	81
WAIST	62	65	64	69
HIPS	76	87	75	84
NECK TO WAIST	33	37	32.5	38
HEIGHT	142	155	137	157

Obviously children in any age-group come in various shapes and sizes, so these measurements are a rough guide only.

Measuring

Take measurements with the person standing straight, and wearing thin garments such as a T-shirt and tights or briefs. However, if making a coat, measure over a thick jumper. Wear the shoes to be worn with the costume, to get the 'length to ground' correct.

CHEST   Measure under arms round fullest part of chest.

WAIST   Tie a piece of string or tape round middle and bend person sideways to make string settle at proper waist; then measure over the string.

HIPS   Measure over fattest part of bottom.

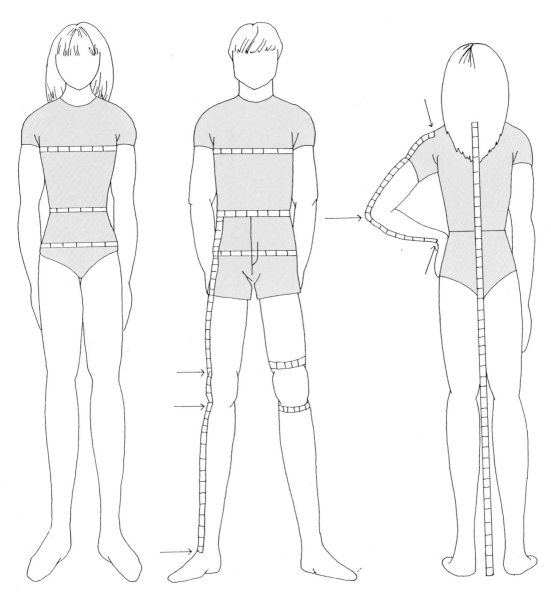

THIGH	Measure where shown on diagram.
KNEE	Measure above or below knee as shown on diagram.
NECK	Measure round base of neck.

Add 2cm to each of the above measurements to allow for ease of fit.

LEG LENGTH	Measure from waist, over hip and down the leg to the required length, as shown on diagram. If measuring to below the knee, add 10cm to allow for sitting down.
NECK TO WAIST	Measure down the back from the base of neck to string marking waist.
NECK TO GROUND	Measure down back from base of neck to ground.
SHOULDER	Measure across the back from base of neck to bone at outer shoulder.
ARM LENGTH	With bent arm, measure from bone at outer shoulder to elbow, then to wrist, as shown in diagram.
ARM GIRTH	Measure round upper arm, forearm, and wrist with finger inside tape to allow for ease of fit.

FITTING GUIDE

Making the pattern

The patterns are all fairly simple shapes, so you may be able to cut them out in the proper material straight away. However, if you are at all doubtful that the costume will fit, it is far safer to first draw out the pattern to full size, on squared paper which is obtainable from dressmaking shops. Then make up the garment first using calico, old sheeting, or other cheap material. You then alter the cheap calico pattern to fit the wearer. Finally you use the calico garment as the pattern on which to cut out the expensive fabric from which the garment is to be made. Think of it in eight stages:

1 Draw pattern to full size on squared paper, adding turnings of 2cm (or as indicated on the specific pattern) on all seams, and 7.5cm on hem. Cut out paper pattern.

2 Pin the paper pattern to calico, and cut out.

3 Using tracing wheel and dressmakers' tracing paper, trace all pattern outlines and markings on to wrong side of calico.

4 Make up according to the specific pattern instructions.

5 Fit the calico garment to the wearer, and mark any necessary alterations. Make sure you fit all parts of the costume in calico *at the same time*; that the armholes and neck are the right size; and that the length of sleeves and hem is correct.

6 When you are quite sure that all the necessary alterations have been marked clearly on the calico, remove it from the wearer and take it apart.

7 Make the alterations carefully, and if you are still not certain of the fit, check it on the wearer again.

8 Now you can use the calico as a pattern for the final version of the garment.

It all sounds rather complicated written down like this. But take it one stage at a time and it should be quite easy. Beginners always want to start making the final costume right away, but a little trouble at this stage might avoid a disaster later!

There are no seam or hem allowances on the patterns, so these must be added when cutting out. All the coats and tunics are meant to fit loosely.

Fabric amounts

It is not possible to give an exact amount of fabric for each costume, as children's measurements vary so much. However, the calico pattern can be measured to give a guide to the amount required. Do not forget to allow more fabric if trying to match patterns or if using a fabric such as velvet where you need to cut everything with the pile running in the same direction. The width of the fabric must also be taken into account.

Egyptian Man and Woman
The man wears a 'loin cloth' and collar. The woman wears a sleeveless tunic and collar.

Assyrian Man
A short tunic with wide sleeves,
over a long sleeveless tunic.

HEBREW MAN

The Hebrew man's costume shown on page 7 could be worn by Joseph in a Nativity play. A plainer version would be appropriate for the shepherds. It is also adaptable for men and boys throughout the Bible stories. He wears a full-length basic tunic with either medium or narrow sleeves. The tunic shown has a decorated front, but you can leave yours plain or decorate it in a different way. Over the tunic he wears a sleeveless open coat, which is also full length. The 'belt' is a length of material wrapped and tied round the waist. The hat is shaped like a flower pot.

Basic tunic

1 Make paper pattern or calico pattern as instructed in Fitting Guide. Then use this paper pattern or corrected calico pattern to cut out fabric.

2 Use a tracing wheel and dressmakers' tracing paper to trace pattern outlines and balance marks on to wrong side of fabric.

3 Right sides together and matching balance marks, join centre back seam from balance mark to hem.

4 Right sides together and matching balance marks, join shoulder seams.

5 Press seams and neaten raw edges.

6 Press seam allowance to wrong side at back opening, and edge stitch. Do not join side seams at this stage.

7 If decorating with facing, cut out facing fabric, adding turnings of 2cm all round.

8 Leaving neck edge raw, turn in remaining edges and pin wrong side of facing to right side of tunic front, matching centre front of facing to centre front of tunic.

9 Stitch together along neck edge seam.

10 Stitch down remaining three sides. A zig-zag machine stitch or an embroidery stitch can be used for a more decorative finish. A

pattern can be drawn on the facing using fabric paints or crayons.

11 Neaten neck edge with bias binding, including raw edge of facing. This can cover the raw edges and show on the right side as decoration, or be turned completely to the inside and stitched down so that it does not show.

12 Fasten centre back neck with a hook and loop, button and loop, or ribbon or tape ties.

13 Attach sleeves as instructed below.

14 Turn up hem and stitch.

Sleeves for coat and tunic

Patterns are given for coat sleeves and tunic sleeves. You can vary the styles of your costumes by using coat sleeves with either coats or tunics. Tunic sleeves are only suitable for tunics, however.

These sleeves are wide with very big armholes, so they will feel a little different to modern sleeves, which usually fit the arms quite closely. It may take a while to get used to all the extra material when you wear the clothes.

Coat sleeves and tunic sleeves are made and attached in the same way.

1 Make paper or calico pattern as instructed in Fitting Guide, adding turnings of 2cm all round. Then use this paper pattern or corrected calico pattern to cut out fabric.

2 Use tracing wheel and dressmakers' tracing paper to trace pattern and balance marks to wrong side of fabric.

ATTACHING SLEEVE

1 Right sides together and matching fold of sleeve 'z' to shoulder seam, join sleeve to tunic or coat from 'x' to 'x'.

2 Press seams, and neaten raw edges.

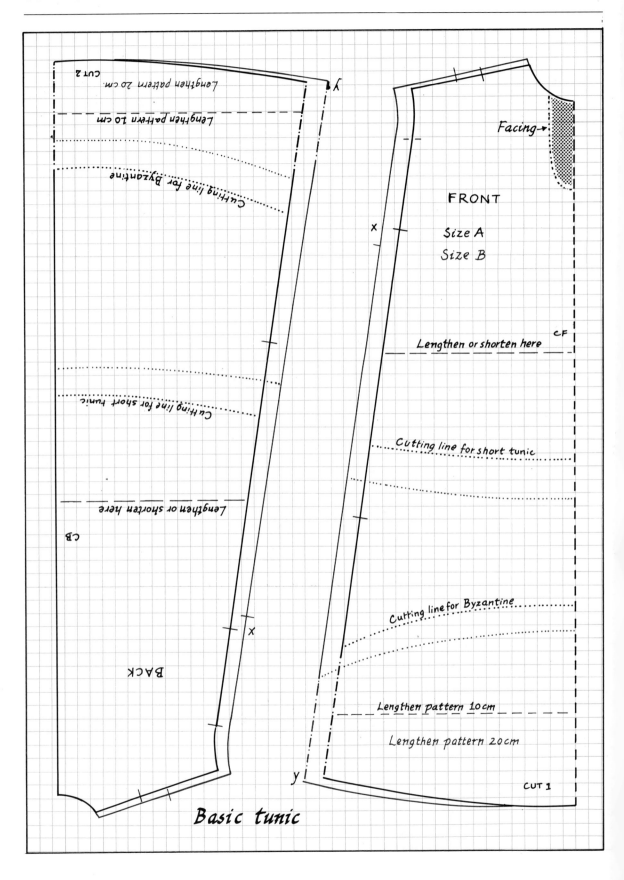

FRONT

Size A

Size B

Facing→

Lengthen or shorten here   CF

Cutting line for short tunic

Cutting line for Byzantine

Lengthen pattern 10 cm

Lengthen pattern 20 cm

CUT 1

Basic tunic

CUT 2   Lengthen pattern 20 cm

Lengthen pattern 10 cm

Cutting line for Byzantine

Cutting line for short tunic

Lengthen or shorten here

CB

BACK

3   Right sides together and matching balance marks, join sleeve and side seams from wrist to hem, clipping into curves if necessary.

4   Press seams and neaten raw edges.

5   Turn up sleeve hem and stitch. This can be done with bias binding.

Basic Coat

All coats in this book are adapted from this pattern. It can have sleeves or be sleeveless. It can be cut to meet at the centre front, or it can be left open. You can add a decorative facing or border, or leave the coat plain.

Sleeveless coat

Cut from the basic coat pattern. Follow the solid lines and ignore the shaded area.

1   Make paper pattern or calico pattern as instructed in the Fitting Guide, adding turnings of 2cm on all seams, 5cm on centre front edges, and 7.5cm for the hem. Then use this paper or calico pattern to cut out fabric.

2   Use tracing wheel and dressmakers' tracing paper to trace pattern outlines and balance marks on to wrong side of fabric.

3   Right sides together and matching balance marks, join shoulder seams.

4   Press seams and neaten raw edges.

5   Neaten raw edges of centre front seam allowance, turn to wrong side, and stitch down. This can be neatened with bias binding.

6   Neaten armhole and neck edges with bias binding, either turned to cover raw edge, or turned completely to inside and stitched down (see Glossary). A contrast binding can give a very decorative finish. The same finish could be used down the front edges of the coat, in which case the turnings should be only 2cm.

7   Turn up hem, and stitch.

To make coat with sleeves, do not neaten armhole edges. Follow instructions for attaching sleeve on page 13.

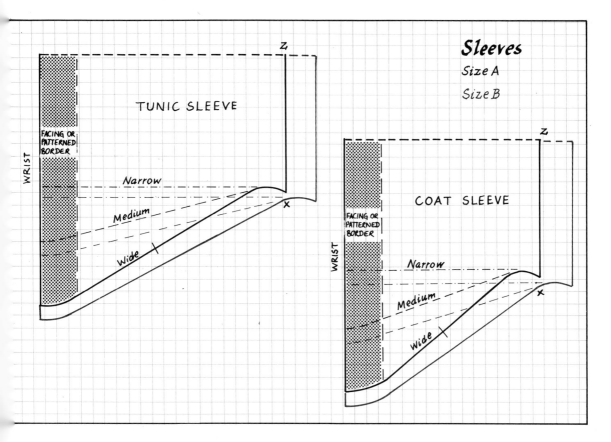

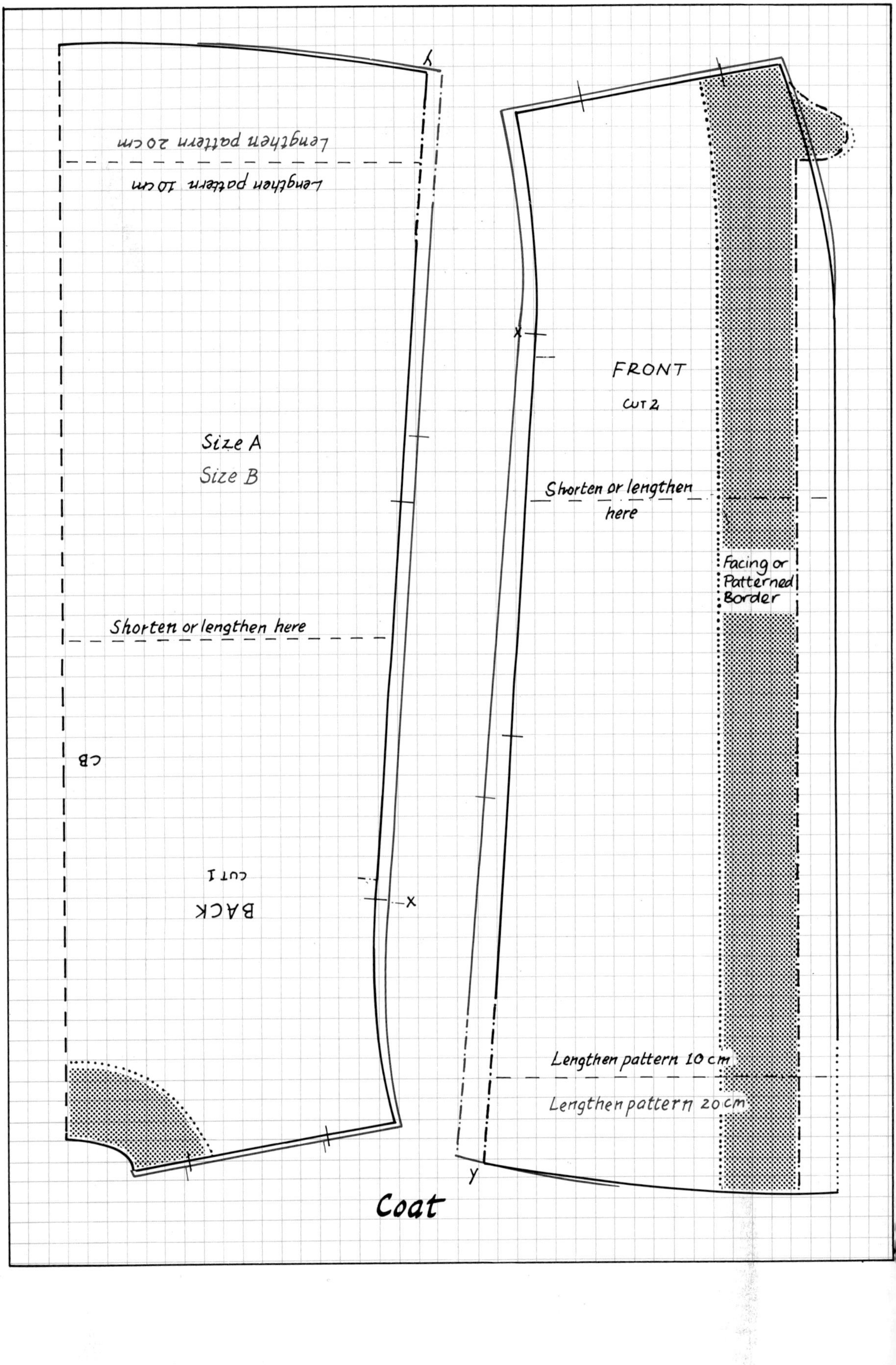

Lengthen pattern 20 cm

Lengthen pattern 10 cm

Size A

Size B

Shorten or lengthen here

CB

BACK
CUT 1

FRONT

CUT 2

Shorten or lengthen
here

Facing or
Patterned
Border

Lengthen pattern 10 cm

Lengthen pattern 20 cm

x

y

Coat

Greek Man and Woman
Both figures wear simple
garments made from squares or
oblongs of material. The
woman's garment is a chiton.

HEBREW WOMAN

The Hebrew woman's costume shown on page 4 could be worn by Mary in the Nativity play and by most other female characters in the Gospel stories. She wears a basic tunic with narrow sleeves. Over this she wears a robe which is gathered at the neck and has elbow-length gathered sleeves. The robe has a decorative facing at the centre front neck. A length of material is wrapped over her head and the ends are thrown over her shoulders. Her belt is another length of material wrapped and tied round the waist.

Tunic

Follow the instructions for making the Hebrew man's tunic and sleeves, and for attaching the sleeves. The only difference is that the woman's tunic does not have a decorative facing. Use the pattern for narrow sleeves below.

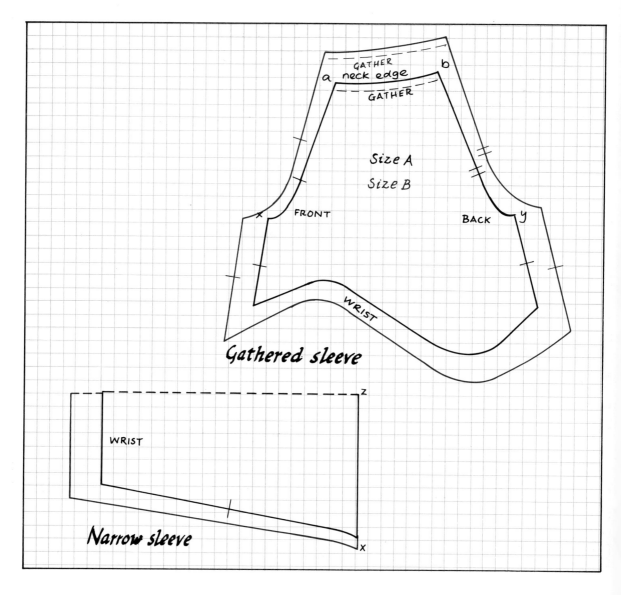

Roman Man and Woman
Both figures wear basic sleeveless tunics. Over the tunic he wears a toga; she wears a short basic tunic without sleeves.

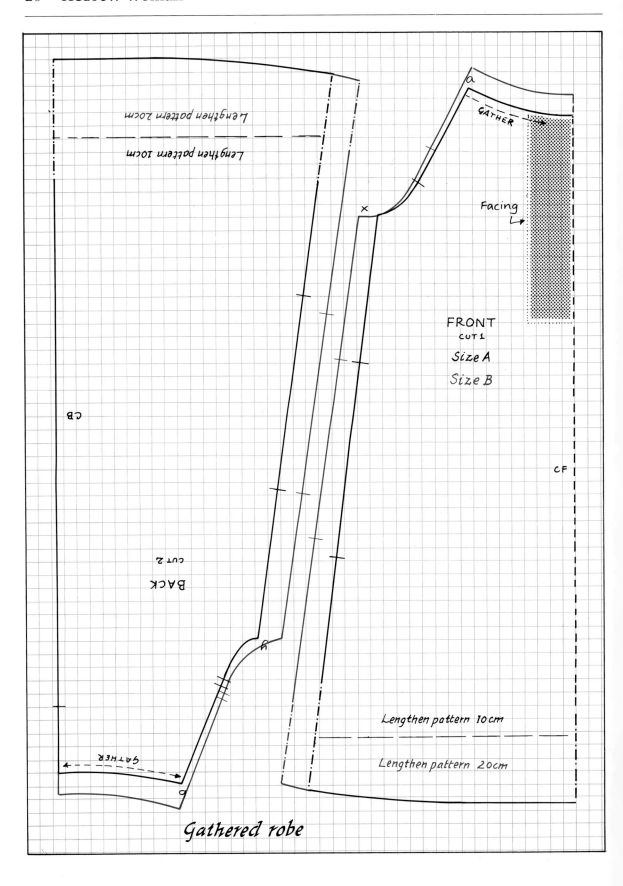

Lengthen pattern 10cm

Lengthen pattern 10cm

Facing

FRONT
CUT 1
Size A
Size B

CB

CF

BACK
CUT 2

GATHER

GATHER

Lengthen pattern 10cm

Lengthen pattern 20cm

Gathered robe

Gathered robe with gathered sleeves

These sleeves are not stitched on afterwards. Front, back, and sleeves are stitched together all at the same time. It is the sleeves which hold the front and back together.

1 Make paper pattern or calico pattern as instructed in Fitting Guide. Then use this paper or calico pattern to cut out fabric.

2 Use tracing wheel and dressmakers' tracing paper to trace pattern outlines and balance marks on to wrong side of fabric.

3 Cut out patterned border, adding 2cm turnings all round.

4 Turn in and pin raw edges, except for neck edge. Wrong side of border to right side of front of robe, stitch together along neck seam. Stitch down remaining three sides. A decorative stitch may be used for this.

5 Right sides together and matching balance marks, join centre back seam. This can be left open from neck to balance mark.

6 If leaving open, neaten raw edges of seam allowance, turn to inside, press, and edge stitch.

7 Right sides together and matching balance marks, join sleeve seams to front armhole seams from 'a' to 'x'.

8 Right sides together and matching balance marks, join back sleeve seams to back armhole seams from 'b' to 'y'.

9 Press seams and neaten raw edges.

10 Right sides together and matching balance marks, join sleeve and side seams from wrist to hem.

11 Press seams and neaten raw edges.

12 Neaten neck edge with bias binding, including neck edge of border and tops of sleeves. Turn binding completely to inside so that it does not show. Leave a gap in binding at centre back to thread elastic.

13 If leaving an opening at back, bind as above, but turn in ends of binding at opening. Stitch down both edges of binding, leaving ends open for threading elastic.

14 Edge stitch.

15 Thread elastic through, pull up until sufficiently gathered and fasten off. A ribbon or tape drawstring could be used instead of elastic.

16 Turn hem at wrist, and stitch. This can be done with bias binding.

17 Turn up hem, and stitch.

EGYPTIAN MAN

The Egyptian couple on page 10 are wealthy and aristocratic. The man's dress would be suitable for, for example, any of the Pharoahs, for Moses as a young man, and for Ptolemy in Shaw's *Caesar and Cleopatra*.

The man's costume opposite we will call a loin cloth, although it was probably not known by this name at the time. A pair of briefs, underpants, or swimming trunks should be used as a foundation. The headdress is made from cardboard, covered with fabric, and decorated in the same way as the collar (page 24); a pattern is not given because it is best to measure the cardboard around the head of the wearer.

Loin cloth

The best type of fabric is cotton lawn, which is a very fine, thin lining material, but any fabric which is soft and drapes well can be used. You could also use finely pleated fabric, but take care when cutting it that you do not stretch the fabric and pull out the pleats. It may not be necessary to make a calico pattern first.

1 Make paper pattern as instructed in Fitting Guide, adding 2cm turnings all round. Then use this paper pattern to cut out fabric.

2 Join centre front seam, neaten raw edges, and press.

3 Turn waist edge to wrong side and stitch down to make a channel for elastic. Leave an opening at back to thread elastic.

4 Edge stitch top edge of waist.

5 Turn and stitch narrow hem along bottom edge.

6 Wrong side facing, lay a length of round elastic down one side of centre front seam. Do not stretch elastic.

7 Make a big knot at top and zig-zag over elastic down centre front, making sure stitches do not catch elastic. Knot bottom end and stitch down very firmly.

8 Repeat down other side of front seam. This zig-zagging can be done over a piping cord. Do not pull elastic or piping cord up yet.

9 Thread elastic through waistband and secure.

FLAP

1 Make paper pattern, adding 0.5cm at bottom and side edges, and 2cm at top. Use pattern to cut out fabric.

2 Zig-zag stitch bottom curve and sides to neaten, or turn and stitch a very narrow hem.

3 Make 2cm pleats right down the length of the flap, as shown on the pattern, and press flat. Stitch along top seam allowance to hold pleats.

4 Gather over piping cord along stitch line.

5 Pull up gathers as tightly as possible, and secure piping cord.

6 Keeping gathers tight, neaten raw edges.

ATTACHING TO FOUNDATION

This should be done on the body to make sure that the garment falls correctly.

1 Put on your foundation of briefs or trunks.

2 Put loin cloth on over foundation.

3 Pull up elastic or piping cord from *top* and fasten off securely.

4 Put on flap, turning waist edge over top of loin cloth and tucking between loin cloth and briefs.

5 Stitch through flap, loin cloth, and briefs to hold all the parts of the garment together. Leave front flap loose to hide stitches.

6 The waist elastic should hold the back of the garment in place. If necessary, catch the back of the loin cloth and briefs together with a few stitches.

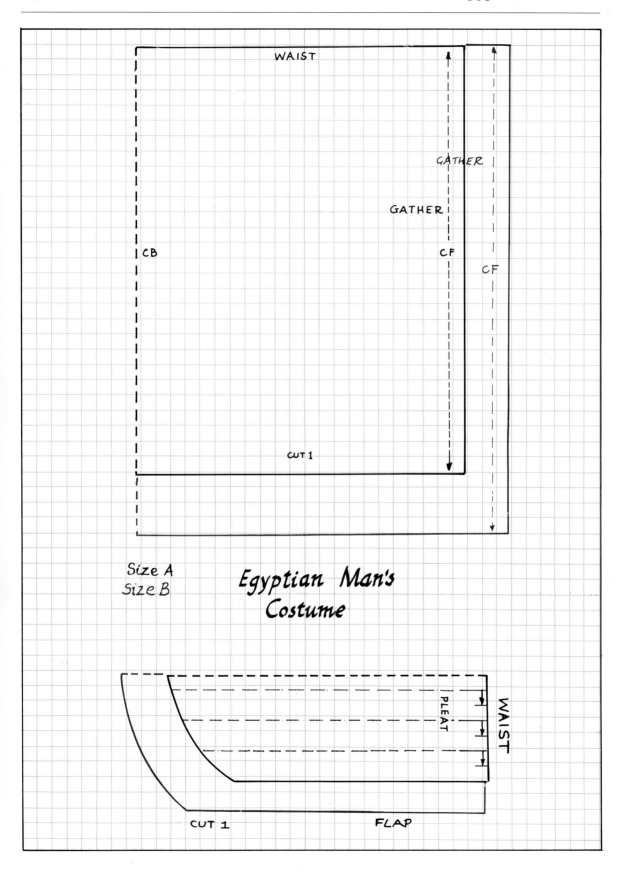

WAIST

GATHER

GATHER

CB

CF

CF

CUT 1

Size A
Size B

Egyptian Man's Costume

PLEAT

WAIST

CUT 1

FLAP

Collar

This should be made in a firm fabric, such as heavyweight calico or canvas, or in felt. If felt is used, the edges should be finished with bias binding to stop it stretching out of shape. You can draw the decoration with felt tip pens, fabric pens or paints. String, ribbon, or wool can be stuck on with a strong glue. Pasta shapes such as macaroni can be painted and stuck on or threaded on string and glued into patterns. You may be able to find beads or broken pieces of jewellery, but if not you can buy them in craft shops. You can paint on glue and sprinkle glitter dust or sequin dust over it. Shake off the excess when the glue is dry.

1   Make paper pattern, adding 2cm turnings all round. Then use this pattern to cut out fabric.

2   Turn and neaten raw edges, clipping into curves, or bind all round.

3   Attach ties at centre back neck.

4   Decorate in any of the ways described above, or decide on your own decorations.

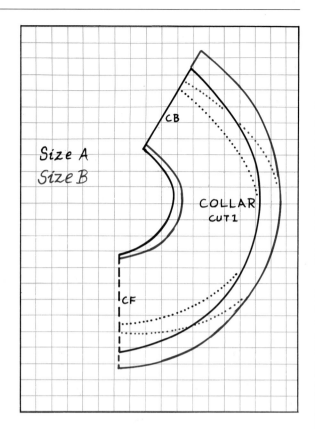

Roman Soldier
A tunic with sleeves, 'skirt', armour, and short cloak.

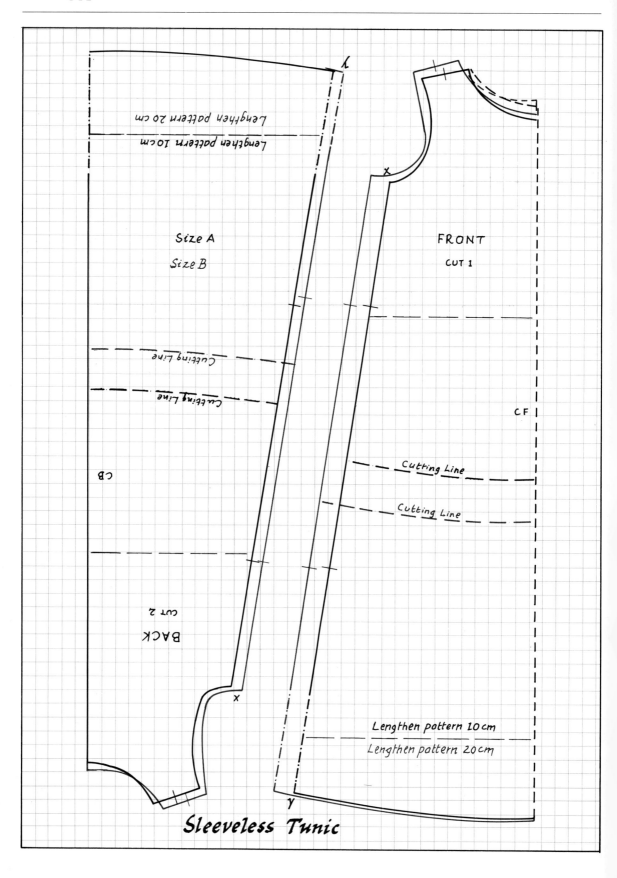

Size A

Size B

FRONT

CUT 1

Lengthen pattern 20 cm

Lengthen pattern 10 cm

Cutting Line

Cutting Line

CF

CB

Cutting Line

Cutting Line

BACK

CUT 2

Lengthen pattern 10 cm

Lengthen pattern 20 cm

Sleeveless Tunic

EGYPTIAN WOMAN

The aristocratic woman on page 10 could be any queen of ancient Egypt, including Cleopatra. Her sleeveless tunic should be made of a soft fabric which drapes well and is not too thick. A pleated fabric would look good, and can sometimes be bought fairly cheaply. Instructions for pleating your own fabric are given on page 8. Her collar is similar to the man's, but the alternative inner cutting line (marked by dots) should be used (see page 24). She wears a headband of beads, ribbon, or fabric.

Sleeveless tunic

1 Make paper pattern or calico pattern as instructed in Fitting Guide. Then use this paper pattern or corrected calico pattern to cut out fabric.

2 Use tracing wheel and dressmakers' tracing paper to trace pattern outlines and balance marks to wrong side of fabric.

3 Right sides together, join centre back seam from balance mark to hem.

4 Right sides together and matching balance marks, join shoulder seams.

5 Right sides together and matching balance marks, join side seam from 'x' to hem.

6 Press seams and neaten raw edges.

7 Press allowance to wrong sides on back opening and edge stitch.

8 Turn allowance to wrong side at neck and armhole, clip into curves, neaten raw edges, and stitch down, *or* neaten neck and armholes with bias binding. Turn binding completely to inside so that it does not show; *or* bind over edge to give a decorative border, in which case, trim away extra fabric to 0.5cm.

9 Fasten neck with tape or ribbon ties, or hook and loop, or button and loop.

10 Turn up hem, and stitch.

ASSYRIAN MAN

The Assyrian warrior in the picture on page 12 is wearing a short tunic with wide sleeves over a long sleeveless tunic. Almost any fabric can be used for this type of costume. Hand-printed material would be particularly effective. You could use potato or lino block prints, or stencils. Some simple instructions for fabric printing are given on page 6 in the Introduction.

It seems that Assyrian costumes were often trimmed with fringing and tassels. These can be obtained from the curtain department of large stores, or from craft shops. The belt is a piece of material trimmed with fringe. The hat is a simple flowerpot shape, trimmed with a piece of twisted fabric; no pattern is given, because it is best to measure it on the head of the person who is to wear it. The leg coverings can be made from leg warmers or footless tights.

Long sleeveless tunic

Cut and make the tunic, following the instructions for the sleeveless tunic worn by the Egyptian woman (page 27). You can trim the bottom hem with fringe, as shown in the picture.

To gather sides, zig-zag over a piping cord down the side seams from the waist to the hem, and pull up to give the effect shown in the picture. Then fasten off securely.

Short tunic

Follow the instructions for the tunic with sleeves worn by the Hebrew man (page 13), using the wide sleeve pattern (page 15). The front can be left plain. The bottom hem should be trimmed with fringe as shown in the picture. Gather the side seams as for the long tunic. Braid or fringe can then be sewn along the gathers to hide the stitches.

The Wise Man, Caspar
A basic tunic, with medium
tunic sleeves with cuffs,
and a cloak.

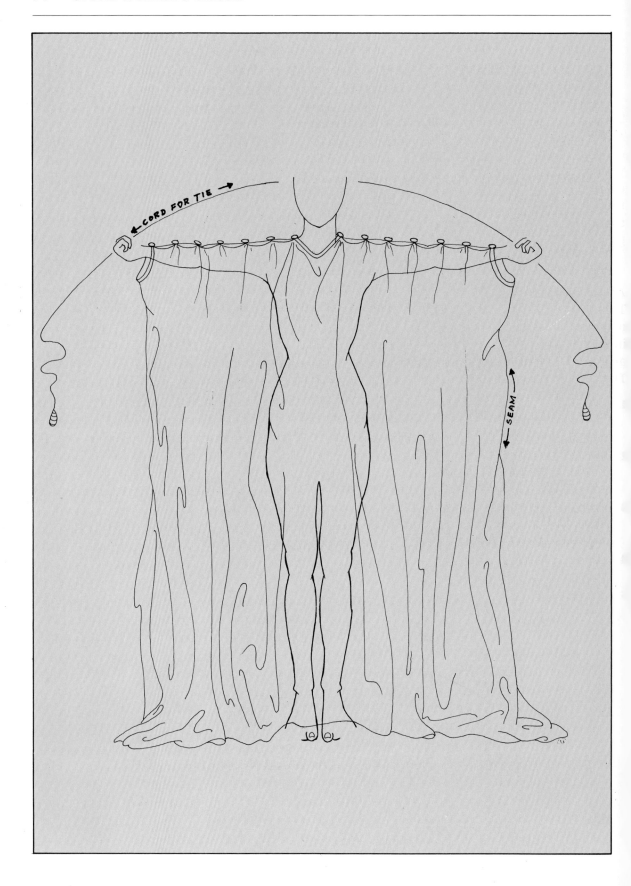

GREEK MAN AND WOMAN

The Greek man and woman on page 17 wear simple garments made from squares or oblongs of material. You should use a lightweight fabric which drapes easily. A light-coloured fabric usually looks best. There are no patterns for these costumes because the shapes are simple. The drawing opposite gives guide-lines for making the woman's chiton.

Man's costume

This costume could have been worn by almost any man in ancient or classical Greece, including Socrates, Alexander, Lysander, and mythological figures like Hercules and Theseus.

1   Measure from back of neck down back to hem length required. Add at least 15cm for draping, and 2cm turnings at top and bottom.

2   Measure across back at shoulder level. Add at least 15cm for draping, and 2cm turnings on each side.

3   Use these measurements to cut two oblongs. If necessary, join fabric to make correct-sized oblong. Press seams and neaten raw edges.

4   Join side seams, leaving a 15cm opening at top for armholes.

5   Press turnings of opening to wrong side, neaten, and edge stitch.

Turn narrow hems at top and bottom. Top edge can be neatened with bias binding.

Leaving a gap for the head, join along the shoulders by stitching, or with buttons or beads and loops.

The tunic can be fastened on both shoulders. To achieve the effect shown in the picture, leave a big gap at the top so that the head and one arm can be slipped through. A tape or ribbon is tied round the waist, and the tunic is pouched over it.

Woman's costume

This costume would be suitable for almost any woman of ancient or classical Greece.

1   Measure from top of head to ground. This is the length of the oblong.

2   With arms outstretched, measure from wrist to wrist across back, and add 2cm for turnings at each side. This is the width of the oblong.

3   Use these measurements to cut two oblong pieces of fabric. If you have to join pieces of material to make a big enough oblong, remember to press seams and neaten raw edges.

4   Right sides together, join side seams to make a large tube.

5   Press seams and neaten raw edges.

6   Turn a narrow hem at bottom.

7   Turn a narrow hem along top edge. You can use bias binding or ribbon for a decorative finish.

8   Join the top edge together at intervals with buttons and loops or beads and loops to give the effect shown in the picture. Leave a large enough gap for the garment to go over the head.

9   Tie a length of ribbon round the waist, or criss-cross ribbon at the back or front. Pouch up the material over it.

ROMAN MAN AND WOMAN

These basic Roman costumes may be adapted for many characters in history, plays, and Bible stories. The man could be Pontius Pilate or any of the Roman emperors. The woman could be Caesar's wife Calpurnia, or Livia the infamous mother of Claudius.

The Romans seem to have worn mostly pale colours. The clothes were made from soft fabrics, which draped. The design on the border of the toga often showed a person's position in society. You may want to copy a particular pattern from a picture. Otherwise, any of the fabric printing ideas given on page 6 could be used to decorate the border.

Woman's costume

The woman is wearing a short, basic tunic without sleeves over a long sleeveless tunic. A ribbon belt is tied slightly above the natural waistline.

Make both the tunics following the instructions for the Egyptian woman's tunic (page 27), but adjust the length as necessary. Use the alternative cutting line for a higher neckline. Roman women also wore togas, and sometimes draped one end over their heads. The toga would probably have been worn over a sleeveless tunic.

Man's costume

The man is wearing a toga over a basic sleeveless tunic.

Make basic sleeveless tunic following the instructions for the Egyptian woman's sleeveless tunic (page 27), but cut to the shorter length.

TOGA

1   A pattern is not given for the toga because it is simply a shaped oblong of material. Follow the diagram when shaping the garment.

2   Use fabric which is at least 122cm wide to avoid making joins. If you do have to join smaller pieces, remember to press seams and neaten raw edges. The long straight edge runs parallel to the selvedge.

3   Turn a narrow hem on all the remaining raw edges. The toga can be draped in many ways. Experiment to find out which style you want.

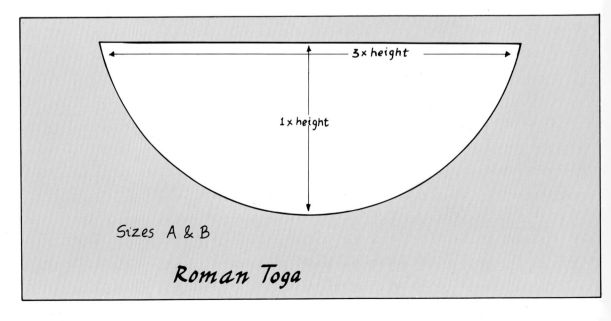

Sizes A & B

Roman Toga

The Wise Man, Balthazar
A basic sleeveless, front-opening
tunic and a coat with narrow
cuffed tunic sleeves.

ROMAN SOLDIER

Roman soldiers conquered a huge area in Europe and the Middle East. Their best-known appearance in the Bible is at the Crucifixion, where a group of them diced for Jesus's coat. The soldier on page 25 wears a tunic with the sleeves and body cut in one piece. Over this he wears a pleated skirt, armour, and a cloak.

Tunic

1   Make a paper or calico pattern as instructed in Fitting Guide. Then use this paper pattern or corrected calico pattern to cut out fabric.

2   Use a tracing wheel and dressmakers' tracing paper to trace pattern outlines and balance marks on to the wrong side of fabric.

3   Right sides together, join centre back seam from balance mark to hem.

4   Right sides together and matching balance marks, join shoulder seams.

5   Right sides together and matching balance marks, join side seams from sleeve end to hem. Clip into curves if necessary.

6   Press seams and neaten raw edges.

7   Press allowance to wrong side at neck opening, and edge stitch.

8   Finish neck with bias binding, and fasten

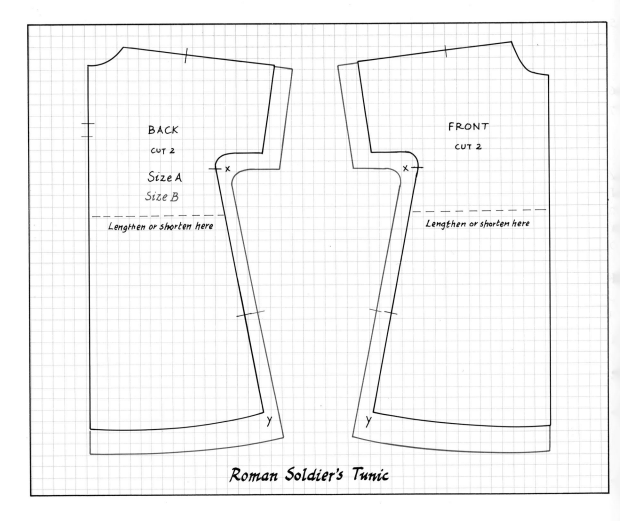

BACK
CUT 2
Size A
Size B
Lengthen or shorten here

FRONT
CUT 2
Lengthen or shorten here

Roman Soldier's Tunic

with tape or ribbon ties, hook and loop, or button and loop.

9 Turn up hem, and stitch.

Skirt

This is simply a length of pleated material, so no pattern is given. The skirt is worn over the tunic and under the knitted armour.

1 Measure the waist over tunic, multiply by 3, and add 4cm for turnings.

2 Measure from waist to length required and add 2cm for waist seam allowance and 5cm for hem.

3 Cut fabric to make an oblong with these measurements. If you have to join pieces of fabric to make a big enough oblong, remember to press seams and neaten raw edges.

4 Centre back seam may be left open, in which case turn back seam allowances to wrong side, neaten raw edges, and stitch down.

5 If closing centre back seam, leave an opening of 20cm and sew up remaining seam. Press seam and neaten raw edges. Edge stitch opening.

6 Turn up hem and stitch.

7 Box pleat waist edge to fit waist measurement over tunic, and finish waist edge as described under Waistband in the Glossary.

Armour

The Roman soldier's armour on page 25 is made from a thick knitted fabric cut to shape. You can also make armour from cardboard, or from synthetic leather material.

KNITTED ARMOUR

Use the pattern for the Egyptian sleeveless tunic (page 27).

1 Make paper pattern as instructed in Fitting Guide.

2 Pin paper pattern to knitted fabric and cut out one piece very carefully.

3 Before cutting out any more, finish raw edges of the cut piece with bias binding to prevent knitting from unravelling. Cut out and bind each piece in this way.

4 Make up as for Egyptian sleeveless tunic.

CARDBOARD ARMOUR

Use strong, thick cardboard and finish with spray paint. The armour does not meet under the arms or on the shoulders. Take measurements over the tunic.

1 Make paper pattern as instructed in Fitting Guide. Mark position of lacing holes.

2 Use paper pattern to cut out cardboard. No turnings are needed.

3 Mark lacing holes on cardboard shapes.

4 Reinforce edges with Sellotape or PVC tape.

5 Stick Sellotape along back of cardboard behind lacing holes.

6 Make lacing holes with a knitting needle or similar pointed instrument.

7 Spray with colour, following the instructions on the can very carefully.

8 Tie armour together with shoe laces or string.

LEATHER-TYPE ARMOUR

Leather-type armour is cut and sprayed in the same way as cardboard. Spray a small piece of the synthetic leather material first, to make sure that the spray is suitable for the material.

1 Make paper pattern as instructed in Fitting Guide, adding turnings of 3cm all around.

2 Mark position of lacing holes.

3 Use paper pattern to cut out fabric very carefully. Use strong scissors.

4 On wrong side, mark seam allowances.

5 Using an all-purpose glue, and following the instructions for the material you are using, turn seam allowances to wrong side and glue down.

6 When glue is dry, make holes, spray if required, and lace as for cardboard armour.

TABS

Tabs are separate flaps of armour, made from the same material, attached to the waist like a very short skirt.

If making tabs in cardboard, cut with no turnings, reinforce, and make as for cardboard armour.

If making tabs in leather-type material,

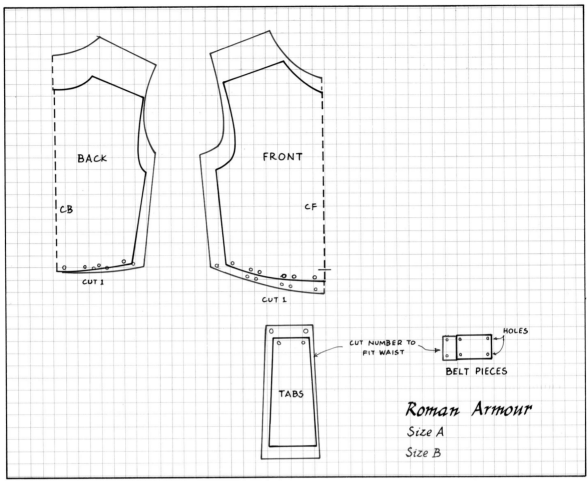

BACK

CB

CUT 1

FRONT

CF

CUT 1

TABS

CUT NUMBER TO
FIT WAIST

HOLES

BELT PIECES

Roman Armour

Size A

Size B

cut with 3cm turnings all round, glue turnings and make up as for leather-type armour. Lace to bottom of armour with shoe laces or string.

Tabs are not necessary with knitted armour.

BELT PIECES

These are made in the same way as the tabs. Remember to measure the waist *over* the tunic, armour, and skirt. Lace the pieces together with shoe laces or string to make a belt. Use the lacing to fasten the belt.

Cloak

The cloak is a half-circle. It is cut and made in the same way as the Byzantine cloak but the Roman cloak is shorter. Use the pattern shown on page 40 but adjust the lines to give the required length. Cut out paper pattern and make cloak as described.

THE THREE WISE MEN

The costumes here are suitable not only for the Wise Men who brought gifts to Jesus, but may be adapted for any wealthy Middle Eastern ruler of Biblical times. They wear variations on the basic tunic and coat patterns already given. Caspar, shown on page 29, wears a basic tunic which has a decorative front opening and medium sleeves with decorative cuffs. His cloak is a square of fabric fastened at the neck by two corners, with the edge drawn up over the head. He wears a headdress shaped like a flower pot, with a piece of twisted fabric round it.

Caspar

1. Make basic tunic pattern as instructed in Fitting Guide. Cut out and trace on balance marks as instructed for Hebrew man's tunic (page 13). Include pattern for medium tunic sleeve.

2. Cut out decorative facing on tunic, using shaded area of pattern, and adding 2cm turnings all round.

3. Right side of facing to wrong side of tunic front, tack together down centre front seam line to 3cm from bottom edge.

4. Stitch 1cm away from tacking line on both sides, and across bottom of tacking line 1cm below bottom stitch.

5. Clip into corners very carefully.

6. Cut along tacking line very carefully.

7. Turn facing to right side and press.

8. Turn in raw edges and stitch into place. A fancy stitch can be used.

9. Right sides together and matching balance marks, join centre back seam and shoulder seams.

10. Press seams and neaten raw edges.

11. Cut out cuffs, using shaded area of tunic sleeve pattern, and adding 2cm turnings all round.

12. Right side of cuff to wrong side of sleeve end, sew together. Press seam open.

13. Right sides together and matching fold of sleeve 'z' to shoulder seam, join sleeve to tunic from 'x' to 'x'.

14. Right sides together and matching balance marks, join cuff, sleeve and side seams from cuff end to hem in one long seam.

15. Turn cuff to right side, turn in raw edge at top and stitch down. You can use the same fancy stitch as for the facing.

16. Turn up hem, and stitch.

Balthazar

Balthazar wears a coat with a decorative facing and narrow cuffed tunic sleeves over a basic sleeveless tunic. His crown could be made of cardboard, with a twisted fabric decoration. The sleeveless tunic is made in the same way as for the Egyptian woman (page 27), but with the neck opening at the front. The neck opening can be neatened with bias binding turned completely to the wrong side so that it does not show, or with a narrow edge showing. A piece of decorative fabric can be cut like bias binding and used in the same way.

COAT

1. Make the basic coat pattern (page 15) from paper or calico as instructed in the Fitting Guide. (Use the alternative cutting line.) Then use this pattern to cut out fabric.

2. Use tracing wheel and dressmakers' tracing paper to trace pattern outlines and balance marks on to wrong side of fabric.

3. Using shaded part of pattern and same cutting line as for coat, cut out front facing to same length as coat front, adding 2cm turnings on side edges.

4. Cut out back facing, adding 2cm turnings.

5. Right sides together and matching balance marks, join shoulder seams of coat.

6 Right sides together and matching balance marks, join shoulder seams of facing.

7 Right side of facing to wrong side of coat, stitch facing to coat up one front, round neck, and down other front.

8 Clip into curves, turn facing to right side, and press.

9 Turn in raw edges and stitch down.

10 Make and stitch on sleeves with cuffs as instructed for Caspar (11–16 on page 37).

11 Turn up hem, and stitch.

12 Fasten with a fancy button and loop or a frog fastening (available from haberdashery departments in stores).

Melchior

Melchior wears a basic short tunic with wide, cuffed sleeves over a basic sleeveless long tunic. He also wears a crown, with twisted fabric. His long sleeveless tunic is made in the same way as for the Egyptian woman's (page 27), but with a decorative front neck opening as for Caspar. His basic short tunic is cut in the same way as the Assyrian short tunic (page 28).

If sleeves with cuffs are preferred, follow the instructions for Caspar's tunic. The bands of decoration can be ribbon, braid or fabric.

The Wise Man, Melchior
A sleeveless long tunic, under
a basic short tunic with wide
tunic sleeves.

BYZANTINE MAN AND WOMAN

After the western part of the Roman Empire fell, the eastern part survived as the Byzantine Empire. It consisted largely of modern Turkey and adjacent parts of Europe.

Man's costume

The Byzantine man wears a basic sleeveless tunic, over which is a short tunic with a shaped hem and medium sleeves. His scarf is a strip of fabric fringed at the ends. It can be shaped at the back of the neck with a small pleat. The scarf is joined at the front with another strip of fabric fastening with a popper or hook and bar. The fabric can be quite bright and patterned. It can be made of painted cardboard or stiffened felt.

The sleeveless tunic is made as for the Egyptian woman (page 27), fastening at the back in the same way. The short tunic is made as for the Hebrew man (page 13), but using the special Byzantine cutting line and medium sleeves.

Woman's costume

The Byzantine woman wears a basic tunic with narrow sleeves, which fastens at the back. Her cloak is a half-circle, fastened to the tunic with a brooch. Her headdress is made in the same way as for the man.

The basic tunic is made as for the Hebrew man (page 13), with back fastening and narrow sleeves.

CLOAK

The neatest way to make this cloak is to use a lining.

1 Make paper pattern as instructed in Fitting Guide, adding turnings of 2cm all round.

2 Use pattern to cut out fabric and lining.

3 Right sides together, stitch lining to fabric all round, leaving a gap to turn cloak inside out.

4 Clip into curves, clip off corners, and turn inside out.

5 Stitch up gap, and press.

6 For an unlined cloak, turn in seam allowances all round, clipping into curves, and stitch down.

7 Fasten at neck with hook, or button and loop, or brooch.

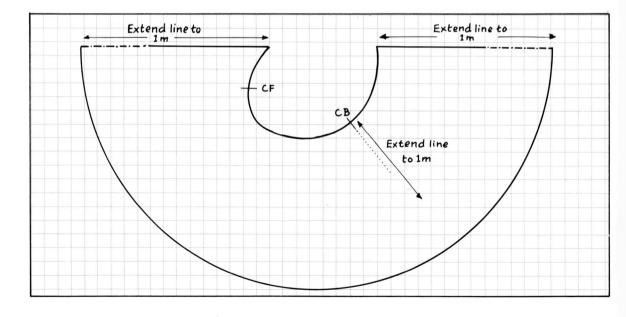

Byzantine Man and Woman
The man wears a basic sleeveless tunic underneath a
short tunic with medium sleeves. The woman wears a
basic tunic with narrow sleeves, and a cloak.

ANGEL

The Angel wears a basic tunic with wide sleeves, made as instructed for the Hebrew man (page 13).

Wings

The wings should be made in cardboard and sprayed an appropriate colour.

1 Make paper pattern as instructed in Fitting Guide. Do not add turnings.

2 Reinforce edges with Sellotape.

3 Mark holes, then reinforce back of holes with Sellotape.

4 Cut holes with point of scissors.

5 Cut 2.5cm elastic and thread through holes. The elastic should cross at the front of the body. Fasten securely at back. Do not pull elastic so tight that it bends the wings.

6 Spray with a suitable colour. Feathers or a pattern can be drawn on with felt tip pens or paints.

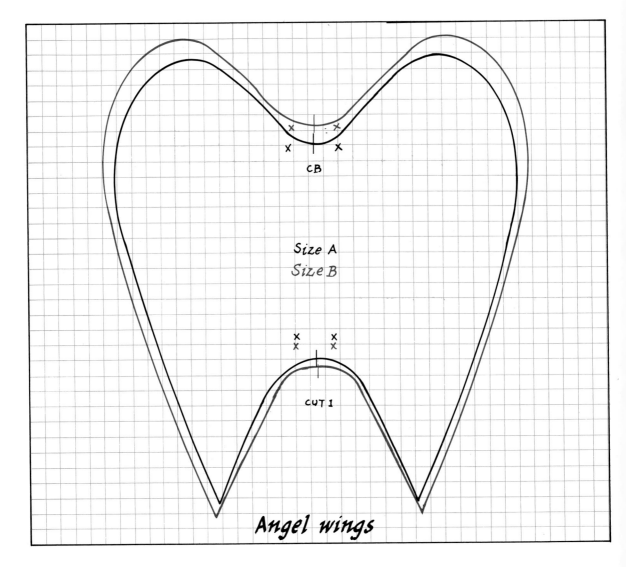

Angel wings

Angel
A basic tunic with wide
sleeves, and wings.

GLOSSARY

BALANCE MARKS Markings on the pattern which are matched so that the separate pieces fit together properly.

BIAS BINDING A type of binding used for turning up and neatening hems and edges.

Open one fold of the binding and pin to right side of hem. Stitch along crease line (diagram A). Then fold to enclose raw edge and stitch (B), or turn completely to inside and stitch (C).

CALICO A cheap cotton material used for pattern-making.

CLIPPING INTO CURVES/CORNERS Cut seam allowance almost to stitch line, about

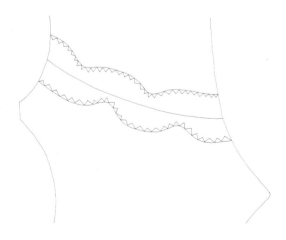

2cm apart, to ease material around curve or corner.

DRESSMAKERS' TRACING PAPER Coloured paper used to transfer information from the pattern to the material. It can be bought in packets with instructions and is used with a spiked tracing wheel.

EDGE STITCH see STITCHES

FACING A way of decorating the edge of a garment.

GATHERING Make a row of stitches each side of the marked line. Pull up to fit measurements and stitch down between rows. If outer row of gathering stitches shows on right side, it can be removed.

HOOKS AND BARS, EYES, OR LOOPS Used for fastening. Set hooks about 2mm from the edge of the material, and sew down firmly through the holes. Sew the hook end down firmly. If using loops, leave the loop protruding over the edge of the material by about 2mm. Stitch down firmly.

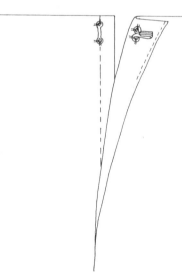

PATTERN See page 8

PETERSHAM A firm tape used for waistbands.

PIPING CORD, GATHERING OVER A Using a wide zig-zag stitch on a sewing machine, zig-zag over the cord. Pull up cord

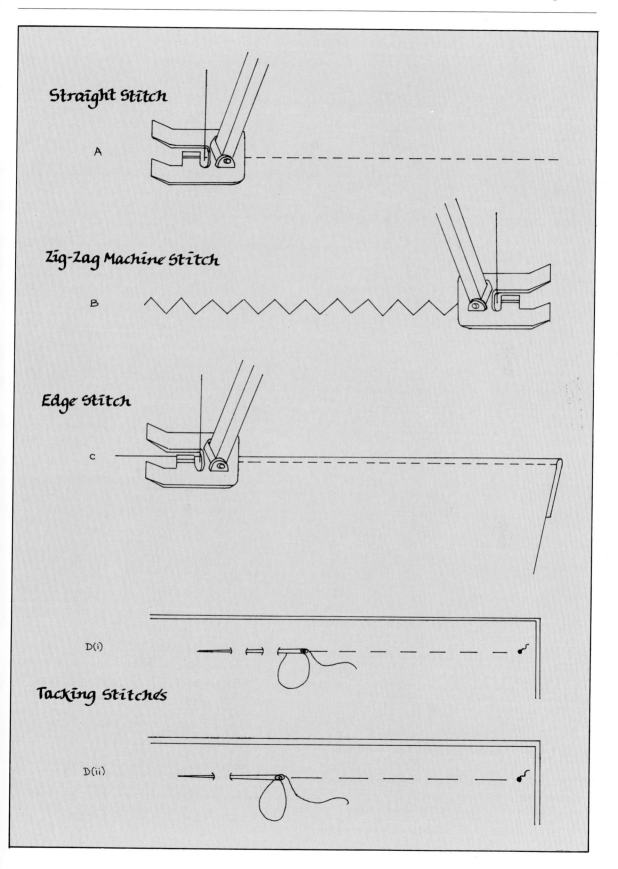

Straight Stitch

A

Zig-Zag Machine Stitch

B

Edge Stitch

C

D(i)

Tacking Stitches

D(ii)

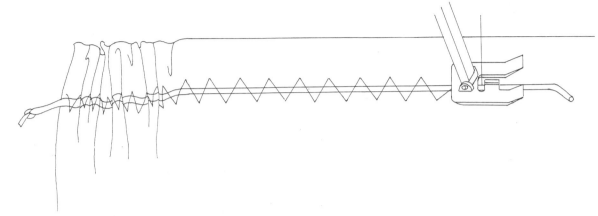

to fit. This is suitable for skirt waists or the heads of very full sleeves.

PLEATS   Flat pleats are all the same width and face the same way. Box pleats consist of two flat pleats turned away from each other. Inverted box pleats consist of two flat pleats facing each other.

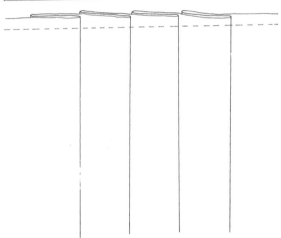

POPPERS   A form of fastening in which one part is snapped into place inside the other.

RAW EDGE   The cut edge of a piece of material.

SELVEDGE   The lengthwise edge of a piece of material (which does not fray).

STITCHES   *Edge stitch*: a row of stitches, usually machined 3mm from folded edge of material to strengthen (c).
Straight stitch: used by hand or machine to join two pieces of material together. Usually for hems and seams (a).
Tacking stitch: used to hold two pieces of material together to be used as one. Also used instead of pinning material together.

Can be short stitches (d1) or long stitches (d2).
Zig-Zag machine stitch: used to neaten raw edges, or over piping cord for gathering (b).

STRAIGHT STITCH   See STITCHES

TABS   See page 35

TACKING STITCH   See STITCHES

WAISTBAND   Usually best made on petersham. Cut to length plus at least 3cm for underlap, plus two 1.5cm turnings. Before making up, sew on two 10cm loops at the sides for hanging up the garment. Sew

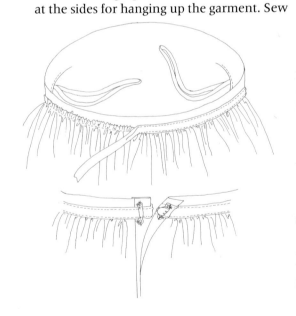

the wrong side of the waist to the petersham (a). Cut off surplus material, turn in seam allowances of petersham and sew on twill or India tape to cover the raw edge. Finish with a trouser hook and bar. The petersham side is next to the body (b).

ZIG-ZAG MACHINE STITCH   See STITCHES

INDEX